Daniel and the Roaring Lions

Daniel 6:1–28 for children
Written by Louise Ulmer
Illustrated by Chris Sharp

ARCH® Books
Copyright © 1996 Concordia Publishing House
3558 S. Jefferson Avenue, St. Louis, MO 63118-3968
Manufactured in the United States of America

When mighty King Darius ruled the ancient world,
His palace in the sands shone like a pearl.
His city called Babylon had gardens in the halls.
Gold-painted lions gleamed on the walls.

Now Daniel the prophet was the king's wisest man,
So Darius put Daniel in charge of his lands.
But certain Persian princes wanted Daniel's place.
They decided to bring Daniel down in disgrace.

So spies watched Daniel all day long,
Hoping to catch Daniel doing something wrong.
But Daniel was honest right down to the penny,
And as for faults, he just hadn't many.

Then one of the spies said, "He has odd ways.
Three times a day Daniel stops and prays.
He goes to his room and gets down on his knees
And prays to a God that no one sees."

The princes went to Darius that very day,
And this is what they asked him to say:
"Make this a law that all must obey:
To foreign gods it's forbidden to pray.
All praise should be given to Darius the king;
It's forbidden to bow before any other thing."

The proud king let the princes have their way
And signed their request into law that day.
The ink on the tablet had just begun to dry,
When his enemies laughed because Daniel would die.

And before the sun had set that day,
The spies arrested Daniel as he knelt to pray.
"Daniel knows the rules and Daniel cheated!
Daniel doesn't pray to the king!" the princes repeated.

Daniel and Darius stood face to face.
"I wish," said the king, "my law we could erase.
There is only one way I can keep the peace.
You will have to go to the den of wild beasts."

Into the lions' pit Daniel was led.
All day the lions had not been fed.
They licked their lips and began to roar,
As outside the king sealed the only door.

With tears in his eyes, the king went away.
In the palace his supper grew cold on its tray.
Only one thing stayed on the sad king's mind.
Would his good friend Daniel be eaten alive?

After listening to the lions roaring all night,
Darius came running as soon as it grew light.
"Daniel!" he shouted. "Please say you're all right!"
Then the king himself almost fainted from fright.

For there stood Daniel, alive and alert.
Amazed, the king shouted, "You're not even hurt!
Oh, Daniel," said the king, "what a great surprise.
Truly your God rules both earth and skies!"

"This day your God has proved to be real,
And before your God my people shall kneel.
Your God saves His people and loves His own.
Let the story of Daniel forever be known."

So remember Daniel in the lions' den—
A true story with a happy end,
For Daniel's God is our God too,
And He always watches over me and you.

Dear Parents:

Children delight in the trickery and bold action in this story. Let them enjoy the story at that level, but help them to also understand that God sends His angels to protect them in all situations. Discuss times when God's angels have obviously been on duty—a close call in the car, an accident while playing, a time when someone has been ill. Pray with your child, thanking God for His loving care and for sending His angels to surround you.

Point out that Daniel prayed boldly to God, even when the king stated that he shouldn't. Talk about the ways you put God first in your family—prayers before meals, reading God's Word at family devotions, budgeting money for church and Sunday school before meeting other needs. Plan something that you can do as a family to make a bold witness—invite neighbors to a family devotion, display a family-made banner celebrating your love for God, make a card for a relative who needs to know Jesus as Savior. Ask God to give you His Holy Spirit's power to always declare your faith in Him, even in difficult situations.

The Editor